Goes with a series

Crash Course Psychology: A Study Guide of Worksheets for Psychology

By Roger Morante

Library of Congress Cataloging-in-Publication Date is available.

ISBN-13: 978-1-7322125-5-8
Writer: Roger Morante
Cover Design: Artwork purchased from 99Designs.com.
Cover Artist: Aaniyah Ahmed
Editor: Roger Morante
Copy Editor: Erica Brown
Back Cover Photo: Liesl Morante
Publisher Logo: Isabella Morante

To contact the publisher, send an email to the address below;
holden713@gmail.com

Additional copies may be purchased on Amazon.com or by contacting the author.

Printed in the United States of America

First printing September 2019

Table of Contents

1) Intro to Psychology: Crash Course Psychology #1
2) Psychological Research: Crash Course Psychology #2
3) The Chemical Mind: Crash Course Psychology #3
4) Meet Your Master- Getting to Know Your Brain: Crash Course Psychology #4
5) Sensation and Perception: Crash Course Psychology #5
6) Homunculus: Crash Course Psychology #6
7) Perceiving is Believing: Crash Course Psychology #7
8) Consciousness: Crash Course Psychology #8
9) To Sleep, Perchance to Dream: Crash Course Psychology #9
10) Altered States: Crash Course Psychology #10
11) How to Train a Brain: Crash Course Psychology #11
12) The Bobo Beatdown: Crash Course Psychology #12
13) How We Make Memories: Crash Course Psychology #13
14) Remembering and Forgetting: Crash Course Psychology #14
15) Cognition – How Your Mind Can Amaze and Betray You: Crash Course Psychology #15
16) Language: Crash Course Psychology #16
17) The Power of Motivation: Crash Course Psychology #17
18) The Growth of Knowledge: Crash Course Psychology #18
19) Monkeys and Morality: Crash Course Psychology #19
20) Adolescence: Crash Course Psychology #20
21) Rorschach and Freudians: Crash Course Psychology #21
22) Measuring Personality: Crash Course Psychology #22
23) Controversy of Intelligence: Crash Course Psychology #23
24) Brains vs. Bias: Crash Course Psychology #24
25) Feeling All the Feels: Crash Course Psychology #25
26) Emotion, Stress, and Health: Crash Course Psychology #26
27) Let's Talk About Sex: Crash Course Psychology #27
28) Psychological Disorders: Crash Course Psychology #28
29) OCD and Anxiety Disorders: Crash Course Psychology #29
30) Depressive and Bipolar Disorders: Crash Course Psychology #30
31) Trauma and Addiction: Crash Course Psychology #31
32) Schizophrenia and Dissociative Disorders: Crash Course Psychology #32
33) Eating and Body Dysmorphic Disorders: Crash Course Psychology #33
34) Personality Disorders: Crash Course Psychology #34
35) Getting Help – Psychotherapy: Crash Course Psychology #35
36) Biomedical Treatments: Crash Course Psychology #36
37) Social Thinking: Crash Course Psychology #37
38) Social Influence: Crash Course Psychology #38
39) Prejudice and Discrimination: Crash Course Psychology #39
40) Aggression vs. Altruism: Crash Course Psychology #40
41) Extra Essay Section

Forward

At the time I was writing this book and studying psychology again in depth, I began to realize everything that was going on around me, and things that I guess I had in previous situations taken for granted. It's like a light bulb went on inside of my head replacing the fog that had been enshrouded in the darkness of my ignorance and forgotten inside of my mind, perhaps lost inside the psychology books that sat scattered around in the bookshelves of my house. Prior to writing Crash Course Psychology: A Study Guide of Worksheets for Psychology, I guess I just used to take everything for granted about people's personalities. I would always say to myself, well, maybe she's just strange or I'm just weird or feeling weird today, and that's why I don't understand her, or him, or even myself. I had it's a not you it's me type of mentality. It's like I never really took the time to reflect and think about human psychology logically, and how it affects all of us both psychologically and physiologically.

Once I started writing Crash Course Psychology: A Study Guide of Worksheets for Psychology, I started reflecting again, really digging in deep as to why people do the things they do and why they experience the emotions they experience and why I experience the emotions that I experience. Then, slowly my reality began starting to make sense, until where I am today.

We humans have a tendency to get stressed out and this stress can end up getting the best of us. But if we learn how to relieve that stress, relieve all those pent-up emotions that cause us pain in our lives, then we will learn to live longer and happier lives. That said, I like to think of human beings as grapes on a vine. And recently I learned that stress is actually good for a grape. When I asked as to why that grape on the vine tasted so good in a wine, I was told that extremes of heat and cold were contributors to that grape tasting so good. Grapes that experienced the most stress that year contributed to that wine being the best vintage year. I believe humans are similar in that respect and if we only learn to heal our minds and bodies from all the stress of life, then we will be able to grow into something beautiful, perhaps more beautiful than if that stress had never been placed upon us in the first place.

Ultimately, by writing this book, the sixth book in my Crash Course workbook series, I learned about the roots of psychology and how it explains the feelings we feel and the emotions that affect and connect all of us inside of this universe that we call home.

So why devote time to Crash Course? Well, many of the questions posed in this workbook actually give students the answers of which the student can then explain in a story or short essay format in the workbook in order to explain the answer to the question. Learning in story fashion, and hybridizing it with videos, affords the mind of the student of Crash Course to think better, remember more, and communicate stronger in their words, thoughts, and actions.

Crash Course Psychology: A Study Guide of Worksheets for Psychology also affords the student a space to write down their emotions and feelings. The student of this book will create their own book reflecting upon the key words and terminology stronger, and design their mind better in order improve communication and understanding in the field of psychology.

In the end peace, calm, and happiness seem to linger inside of my body whenever I seem to figure it all out. It is my goal to share this energy and help people understand how to be able to communicate more effectively using the vocabulary of psychology to explain to each other the wonders of the human mind and how our interaction on this planet affects us all.

Name____________________
Period___________________
Date_____________________

Intro to Psychology-Crash Course Psychology #1

1) Briefly explain how the origins of **psychology** relate to the study of psychology today.

____
____
____
____
____
____

2) Create four questions that you believe most epitomizes what the **field of psychology** attempts to solve.

A) ____
____

B) ____
____

C) ____
____

D) ____
____

3) Evaluate the reasons why psychologist **Sigmund Freud** (1856-1939) was one of the most **influential** and **controversial** thinkers of his time and even our time.

____
____
____
____
____
____

4) Analyze the origins of the **field of psychology** in relation to its focus on **structuralism**, **functionalism**, and **psychoanalysis**:

a) **Structuralism** -Edward Bradford Titchener (1867-1927)

____
____
____
____

b) **Functionalism** -The Principles of Psychology, William James (1842-1910)

____
____
____
____

c) **Psychoanalysis** -The Interpretation of Dreams, Sigmund Freud- **free association**

____

____

____

____

____

____

5) Evaluate the merits behind Freud's theory that the **subconscious** could be understandable through **psychoanalysis**. *Include why this concept of understanding changed the* ***field of psychology***.

____

____

____

____

____

____

6) Explain what happened to **Sigmund Freud** in the later years of his life. *Include the* ***social, political****, and* ***economic*** *factors shaping the later years of his life in your answer.*

____

____

____

____

____

____

____

7) Explain how the contributions of Ivan Pavlov (1849-1936), John B. Watson (1878-1958), and B.F. Skinner (1904-1990) redefined **psychology** under the banner of **observable behavior**.

____

____

____

____

____

____

____

8) Briefly explain how **psychodynamic** theories aid in understanding how a person's **unconsciousness** affects their **thoughts**, **feelings**, and **personality**.

____

____

____

____

____

____

Name___________________
Period__________________
Date___________________

Psychological Research-Crash Course Psychology #2

1) Explain how a person's **intuition** can lead to **overconfidence** and sometimes be wrong leading to **hindsight bias**.

____
____
____
____
____

2) Analyze how **scientific inquiry** aids people in understanding **psychology**, aka (also known as) the study of our minds.

____
____
____
____
____

3) Explain how the **scientific method** works hand in hand by utilizing an example that expresses a clear and common language in order so that YOU can think better.
   a) **Question**, and a **theory**

   ____
   ____

   b) **Hypothesis**, testable **prediction**

   ____
   ____

   c) **Test** with a replicable **experiment**

   ____
   ____

4) Draw conclusions as to why is it important to have **case studies** when formulating a **hypothesis**.

____
____
____
____
____

5) Clarify why the **naturalistic observation** approach to describing one's **behavior** is key to the understanding of that person's **psychology**.

____
____
____
____

6) Explain the **limitations** of the research of Alfred Kinsey (1894-1956) which used surveys to access a person's consciously held **attitudes** and **beliefs**. *Include how his work could have **sampling bias** attached to it.*

7) How can a psychologist use **random sampling** in understanding how certain **traits** or **behavior** are related to each other?

8) Clarify the reasons why a psychologist would run an **experiment**.

9) Explain the differences between a **control group** and an **experimental group**. *Include how the use of a **placebo** can be used to analyze **data**.*

10) Draw conclusions as to how **bias** can ruin an **experiment**.

Name___________________
Period__________________
Date____________________

The Chemical Mind-Crash Course Psychology #3

1) Compare the differences inside a **neuron** between **dendrites**, the **cell body**, and **axons**.

____
____
____
____
____
____
____
____
____

2) Explain how **multiple sclerosis** damages the **sheaths of nerve cells** in the **brain** and the **spinal cord**.

____
____
____
____
____
____

3) Differentiate between the **synaptic gap**, the **synapse**, and the **receiving neuron**. *Be sure to explain what happens when an **action potential** runs down to the **axon terminal** inside of your answer.*

____
____
____
____
____
____
____

4) Explain how **neurotransmitters** connect with their intended **receptors** to deliver information, but not stay attached to their **host neuron**.

____
____
____
____
____
____
____

5) Briefly explain how the **communication of neurons**, along with the help of **neurotransmitters**, cause **motion** and **emotion**.

____
____
____
____
____

6) Clarify the role **endorphins** play in causing **human emotions** such as **pain** and **pleasure**.

____
____
____
____
____

7) Explain the function of **excitatory neurotransmitters** such as **norepinephrine** and **glutamate**. *Include how YOU think they rev* ***neurons*** *up.*

____
____
____
____
____

8) Clarify what causes people to be sensitive to **MSG** (**monosodium glutamate**) inside of Chinese food with the resulting effect of that **consumption** to include **migraines** and possible **seizures**.

____
____
____
____
____
____

9) Describe how **inhibitory neurotransmitters** chill **neurons** out.

____
____
____
____
____

10) Differentiate between the functions of **hormones** in the **endocrine system** and **neurotransmitters** in the **brain**.

____
____
____
____
____
____
____

11) Evaluate the advantage of having **adrenal glands** to elevate your **heartrate** and **blood pressure** when YOU are in a "fight or flight" mode. *Analyze a time when this happened to YOU in order to strengthen understanding.*

12) Analyze the function of the **pancreas** which oozes **insulin** and **glucagon hormones** and is located next to the **adrenal glands**.

13) Analyze the function of the **thyroid** and **parathyroid glands** which are located at the base of your **throat**.

14) Compare the differences between **testosterone** in **males** and **ovaries** in **females**.

15) Explain why the **pituitary gland** is the most influential **gland** in the **endocrine system**.

16) Briefly analyze what happens during the **chain of command** in order to explain how somebody sees something and ultimately reacts to it.

17) Clarify what is going on in the **feedback loop** inside of your body.

Name___________________
Period__________________
Date___________________

Meet Your Master-Getting to Know Your Brain: Crash Course Psychology #4

1) Explain the reasons why YOU think **phrenologist** Franz Joseph Gall (1758-1828) was wrong in his studies of **phrenology** in his conclusion that different **skull** shapes lead to differences in intelligences.

____
____
____
____

2) Explain how Gall's research reshaped the way **psychologists** think about the **brain** today with different parts of the **brain** controlling specific aspects of our **behavior**, *i.e. vision, movement, memory, speech, and facial recognition.*

____
____
____
____

3) Analyze how the **central nervous system (CNS)**, or the command center of the body, is different from the **peripheral nervous system**.

____
____
____
____
____
____

4) Recount the importance of railroad worker Phineas Gage (1823-1860), who survived his head impaled by a metal rod, in understanding the importance of how the **brain** works.

____
____
____
____
____
____

5) Point out and explain the misnomer that people only use 10% of their **brain** and that people might be able to live normally without parts of the **brain** or even the other 90%.

____
____
____
____
____
____

6) Analyze and evaluate the differences in function between the **brains** of **less complex** animals and the **brains** of **more complex** animals.

____

____

____

____

____

____

7) Differentiate between the **regions** of the outer portions of the **brain** and the **regions** of the inner core of the **brain**, i.e. old brain, brain stem, medulla, pons, thalamus, reticular formation, cerebellum.

   a) **Old brain**:

   ____

   ____

   b) **Brain stem**:

   ____

   ____

   c) **Medulla**:

   ____

   ____

   d) **Pons**:

   ____

   ____

   e) **Thalamus**:

   ____

   ____

   f) **Reticular Formation**:

   ____

   ____

   g) **Cerebellum**:

   ____

   ____

   ____

8) Differentiate between the functions of the **limbic system**. i.e. **amygdala**, **hypothalamus**, **hippocampus**, and **pituitary gland**.

   a) **Amygdala**:

   ____

   ____

   b) **Hypothalamus**:

   ____

   ____

   c) **Hippocampus**:

   ____

   ____

d) **Pituitary gland**:

9) Point out and explain the differences between the **right** and **left hemispheres** of the **brain** which are connected by the **corpus callosum**.

10) Explain what is meant by the behavior disorder known as **pop psychology**.

11) Briefly analyze the function of the **cerebral cortex**.

12) Clarify the function of **glial cells**.

13) Briefly analyze the function of the **four lobes** of the **cerebral cortex**.

a) **Frontal Lobe**:

b) **Parietal Lobe**:

c) **Occipital Lobe**:

d) **Temporal Lobe**:

Name____________________
Period__________________
Date____________________

Sensation and Perception: Crash Course Psychology #5

1) Analyze how **sensing** and **perceiving** are connected but different, taking into account the **neurological disorder** of **prosopagnosia** experienced by Dr. Oliver Sacks (1933-2015).

____
____
____
____
____
____
____

2) Analyze the role that the **absolute threshold** of **sensation** plays in YOUR daily life.

____
____
____
____

3) Analyze the model for **signal detection theory** and use it to explain why new parents might hear their baby's tiniest cry but not hear the roar of a passing freight train.

____
____
____
____

4) Formulate a theory surrounding **sensory adaptation** and an item of choice that YOU carry around daily.

____
____
____
____
____
____

5) Explain **phenomena** in terms of concepts using **Weber's Law** to evaluate how **difference threshold** in **perception** is NOT **linear**.

____
____
____
____
____
____
____

6) Explain how **vision** works by clarifying how **light** refracts inside of your eyeball in order to create an **image of perception** in your mind.

7) Differentiate between **light** that has **short wavelengths** and **light** that has **long wavelengths** in relation to **human perception**.

8) Investigate how the **retinal receptors** of **rods** and **cones** aid in **human vision**.

9) Briefly explain the hallmarks surrounding how the **Young-Helmholtz Trichromatic Theory** works in relation to **human vision**.

10) Differentiate between **dichromatic** and **trichromatic vision**.

11) Analyze how the **opponent-process theory** works to aid people to see in **color**.

12) Examine the **biology** behind how a human **eyeball** sends signals to the **brain** so that an individual can see in **color**.

13) Explain how **object perception** works to aid a person who can't recognize human faces but still has the ability to pick their keys off a pile on a counter.

14) Explain how **parallel processing** allows a person to process and analyze many different aspects of a **situation** at once.

15) Briefly assess how **visual processing** allows the **brain** to simultaneously make sense of **form**, **depth**, **motion**, and **color**.

Name____________________
Period__________________
Date____________________

Homunculus: Crash Course Psychology #6

1) Briefly analyze how **homunculus** is related to how our bodies react with the **environment**.

____
____
____
____

2) Explain how our **eyes** and **ears** function to provide us with both **sensations** and **perception**.
A) **Eyes**

____
____
____
____
____
____

B) **Ears**

____
____
____
____
____
____
____
____

3) Analyze how **taste buds** inside of a **tongue** detect five distinct **tastes**: sweet, salty, sour, bitter, and umami.

____
____
____
____
____

4) Give an example and then analyze **sensory interaction** when using your **olfactory senses**, aka sense of smell.

____
____
____
____

5) Explain how the rare **neurological** condition of **synesthesia** causes two or more **senses** to get wrapped together and stimulate different parts of the body.

____

____

____

____

6) Evaluate the differences between three of the current **theories** as to why people experience **synesthesia**.

____

____

____

____

____

____

____

7) Explain how our minds detect the **chemical senses** of **taste** and **smell**.

____

____

____

____

____

____

8) Draw conclusions as to how certain **smells** may conjure up **memories** by analyzing an example of choice.

____

____

____

____

____

9) Draw conclusions as to why the **sense of touch** is extremely important early in **human development**.

____

____

____

____

____

____

10) Analyze the four different types of **skin sensations**: pressure, cold, warmth, and pain.

____

____

____

____

____

Name__________________
Period_________________
Date__________________

Perceiving is Believing: Crash Course Psychology #7

1) Evaluate how our expectations in our **perceptual set** influence what we see in our mind regardless of what we see with our **eyes**.

____
____
____
____
____
____
____
____

2) Explain how context and expectations, as well as culture, are factors in your **perceptual set** in determining how your **brain** interprets an **image**.

____
____
____
____
____

3) Show how your personal **perceptual set** can lead you not only to reasonable conclusions but can also be misleading or even harmful.

____
____
____
____
____

4) Analyze how **form perception** allows our minds to understand shape and form, depth, color, movement, and contrast and ultimately form a **figure-ground relationship**.

____
____
____
____
____

5) Analyze the "faces or vases" **illusion** example in order to better understand the **figure-ground relationship**.

____
____
____
____
____

6) Examine how **non-visual fields** such as focusing in on that certain someone at a party allow us to understand the **figure-ground relationship** of a person's **perception**.

7) Explain how **proximity**, **continuity**, and **closure** aid our minds in making sense of all the shuffling stimuli in order to create a coherent and understandable picture.

8) Evaluate what would happen if you did not have any **depth perception**.

9) Analyze how **retinal disparity** such as **binocular cues** and **monocular cues** aid in **depth perception**.

10) Explain how our **interposition**, or **overlap cues**, inform us about the **proximity** of an object.

11) Explain how **motion perception** can infer the speed and direction of a moving object.

12) Briefly explain how **perceptual constancy** allows us to recognize an object regardless of its distance, viewing angle, motion, or illumination.

Name___________________
Period__________________
Date___________________

Consciousness: Crash Course Psychology #8

1) Explain how psychologist **William James** (1842-1910) saw **consciousness** as continually moving such as defined in the term **stream of consciousness**.

____
____
____
____
____

2) Analyze how **consciousness** allows us to think about life.

____
____
____
____

3) Evaluate what YOU think it means to really be **awake**.

____
____
____
____
____

4) Explain how **brain activity** links with our **mental process** in the field of **cognitive neuroscience**.

____
____
____
____
____
____

5) Apply concepts to understand the differences between the two types of **imaging**:
   a) **structural imaging**

   ____
   ____
   ____
   ____

   b) **functional imaging**

   ____
   ____
   ____
   ____

6) Defend the theory of **dual processing** that states that humans don't just have **one layer** of **consciousness** but **multiple layers** of **consciousness**.

7) How does **selective attention** focus the human mind so that humans can actually get things done throughout the day? *Defend your argument with an example or two.*

8) Analyze the **cocktail party effect** and how it relates to hearing your name.

9) Analyze what could happen if you activate your **selective inattention** while texting and driving, and then come down with **inattentional blindness**.

10) How do **magicians** use misdirection along with **inattentional blindness** and **change blindness** to fool people from what was there a moment ago to what is there now?

11) Explain what happened during the psychological experiment known as the **person swap**.

Name___________________
Period_________________
Date___________________

To Sleep, Perchance to Dream: Crash Course Psychology #9

1) Assess what it means to **sleep** and why YOU think that there hasn't been a **scientific consensus** as to why humans need to sleep.

____
____
____
____
____
____

2) Analyze how the **endocrine system** changes its function from when a person is awake to when a person falls asleep as determined from an **EEG** (**Electroencephalogram**) reading.

____
____
____
____
____
____
____

3) Differentiate between the four distinct stages of sleep: NREM-1 (Non-REM-1), NREM-2, NREM-3, Full REM (Rapid Eye Movement).
   a) **NREM-1** (hypnagogic sensations)

   ____
   ____
   ____

   b) **NREM-2** (sleep spindles)

   ____
   ____
   ____

   c) **NREM-3** (delta waves, broken dreams)

   ____
   ____
   ____
   ____

   d) **Full REM** (vivid dreams)

   ____
   ____
   ____
   ____

4) Briefly evaluate the **health problems** that could occur to a person's body due to **sleep deprivation**.

____

____

____

____

5) Differentiate between different **sleep disorders** which could cause havoc inside of a person's life:

   A) **Insomnia** -Difficulty falling asleep or staying asleep-

   ____

   ____

   ____

   ____

   B) **Narcolepsy** – falling asleep in relaxing surroundings- hypocretin irregularities

   ____

   ____

   ____

   ____

   C) **Sleep apnea** -breathing repeatedly starts and stops while asleep

   ____

   ____

   ____

   ____

   D) **Case of Mike Birbiglia** (1978-present) -dopamine deficiency

   ____

   ____

   ____

   ____

   E) **Night terrors** (NREM-3) -stress at night-most common in children under seven

   ____

   ____

   ____

6) Why do YOU think people dream? *Cite examples from competing theories about the nature of* ***oneirology*** *to help back up your claim in your answer.*

____

____

____

____

____

____

____

____

____

Name___________________
Period_________________
Date___________________

Altered States: Crash Course Psychology #10

1) Analyze Franz Mesmer's (1734-1815) contribution to the scientific field of **hypnosis** and **altered states of consciousness** even though he was discredited from his own **scientific community**.

____
____
____
____
____
____

2) Assess the phenomenon of **hypnosis** by showing how YOU think it could be effective in treating stress, anxiety, weight loss, and chronic pain.

____
____
____
____
____
____

3) Analyze a reason why YOU think only 20% of the population seems to be **hypnotizable**.

____
____
____
____
____
____

4) Explain the popular **social influence theory** which believes that the phenomenon of **hypnosis** increases if the subjects treat their **hypnotist** as a director of a movie or play.

____
____
____
____
____
____

5) Explain the special **dual-processing theory** which focuses on the **dissociation** of the subject during the phenomenon of **hypnosis**.

____
____
____
____

6) Synthesize how **dissociation** could help YOU or has helped YOU face a dangerous situation which requires a quick and reflexive action.

7) Evaluate how **hypnosis** allows some people to tap into their **adaptive dissociative capacity**.

8) Construct a good reason as to why a person's body and mind might build a tolerance to drugs that alter their **state of mind**.

9) Prove how **tranquilizers** or **barbiturates** depress the **nervous system**.

10) Draw conclusions as to how **stimulants** could be prescribed by a doctor for somebody who suffers from **anxiety** or **insomnia**.

11) Develop a logical argument as to why it is probably not a good idea to become addicted to **opiates** such as **heroin** or **morphine**.

____

____

____

____

____

____

12) Investigate what **cocaine** does to the **brain** after it hits the bloodstream.

____

____

____

____

____

____

13) Explain how **methamphetamine** excessively activates **neurotransmitters** in the **brain** after it hits the bloodstream.

____

____

____

____

____

____

____

14) Analyze how **hallucinogens** react inside the **human mind** to cause **neurological hallucinations**.

____

____

____

____

____

____

____

15) Explain the **phenomena** of people reporting **auditory hallucinations** in times of emergencies without the use of **hallucinogenic drugs**.

____

____

____

____

____

____

____

____

Name____________________
Period___________________
Date____________________

How to Train a Brain: Crash Course Psychology #11

1) Prove how Ivan Pavlov 's (1849-1936) work on **behaviorism** was tremendous and led to the foundation of the **Behaviorist School of Thought**.

____
____
____
____
____

2) Briefly explain how **associative learning** can be acquired through **association**, **observation**, or **thinking** so that a **neutral-stimuli** -such as a sound or a light- can stimulate an **observable reaction**.

____
____
____
____
____

3) Break down and analyze the sequence of steps inside of Pavlov's famous dog experiment in order to understand how **classical conditioning** works through **associative learning**.

____
____
____
____
____
____

4) Evaluate the contribution to the field of **behavioralist psychology** of **psychologists** B.F. Skinner (1904-1990) and John B. Watson (1878-1958), author of Behaviorism (1912).

____
____
____
____
____

5) Compare the differences between **classical conditioning** and **operant conditioning**.

____
____
____
____
____
____

6) Describe the purpose of an invention called the **air crib** by B.F. Skinner.

7) Analyze how a box provided an **observable stage** for a rat to demonstrate Skinner's concepts of **positive reinforcement** through **operant shaping**.

8) Compare the merits of **positive reinforcement** against the merits of **negative reinforcement**.

9) Clarify the differences between **negative reinforcement** and **punishment**.

10) Explain how we are taught (or **conditioned**) to behave in certain ways in order to get what we want or don't want through **primary reinforcers**. *Provide an example from YOUR OWN life of this.*

11) Briefly explain how receiving a **paycheck** is an example of a **conditioned reinforcer**.

Name____________________
Period__________________
Date____________________

The Bobo Beatdown: Crash Course Psychology #12

1) Explain why kids were more likely to take out their frustration and mimic aggression in Albert Bandura's (1925-present) **clown punching bag experiment** after seeing an adult display aggression towards a clown doll.

____
____
____
____
____

2) Investigate how Bandura's views challenged the **status quo** surrounding the **behaviorist theory** of **conditioning** and **association** in the early 1960s.

____
____
____
____
____

3) Analyze how **pure behaviorism** added new dimensions to the models of **social-cognitive learning**.

____
____
____
____
____
____

4) Explain how **associative learning** occurs when a subject links together certain events, stimuli, or behavior together in the process of **conditioning** by analyzing an example of choice.

____
____
____
____
____

5) Compare **classical conditioning** to **operant conditioning**.

____
____
____
____
____
____

6) Develop a logical argument as to why critics would have trouble with the assertions of Pavlov, Watson, and Skinner in the field of **Behavioral Psychology**.

____

____

____

____

____

7) Explain why **learned associations** are more complicated in humans than in animals.

____

____

____

____

____

____

8) Analyze why YOU think **cognition** and **social context** are important for learning.

____

____

____

____

9) Evaluate a scenario where YOU experienced **latent learning** by using **cognitive maps**.

____

____

____

____

____

____

10) Cite evidence as to how YOUR own **observational learning** and **modeling** can influence YOUR behavior.

____

____

____

____

____

____

11) Analyze a scenario in which **neuroimaging** can show the **reward pathway** of a person's brain light up due to the existence of **mirror neurons**.

____

____

____

____

____

____

Name____________________
Period___________________
Date____________________

How We Make Memories: Crash Course Psychology #13

1) Formulate a theory as to how YOUR **memory** works (or doesn't work) so that YOU can remember to brush YOUR teeth every night.

____
____
____
____
____

2) Assess the three ways in which our **memories** are typically accessed:
   a) **Recall** (___________, Greece)

   ____
   ____
   ____

   b) **Recognition** (multiple choice)

   ____
   ____
   ____

   c) **Relearning** (reinforcement)

   ____
   ____
   ____

3) Explain the processes behind the three stages of memory formation that Richard Atkinson (1929-present) and Richard Shiffrin (1942-present) figured out in the 1960s:
   a) **Sensory memory**

   ____
   ____
   ____
   ____

   b) **Working/short-term memory**

   ____
   ____
   ____
   ____

   c) **Long-term memory storage**

   ____
   ____
   ____
   ____

4) Evaluate the reasons why later generations of psychologists revisited the idea of **short-term memory** and updated it to the more comprehensible concept of **working memory**.

5) Compare the differences between **explicit memory** and **implicit memory**.

6) Explain how **automatic processing** is done without conscious effort.

7) Compare the differences between **procedural memory** and **episodic memory** when it comes to **long term memory** storage in the brain.

8) Assess how **mnemonics** and **chunking** can help YOU memorize and remember the colors of the rainbow or somebody's telephone number.

9) Explain how different kinds of processing can decide how well you retain a **memory**.

Name___________________
Period__________________
Date____________________

Remembering and Forgetting: Crash Course Psychology #14

1) Develop a logical argument as to why it takes a lot of work to retrieve **memories** from long-term storage in our brains and **remember** things that have happened.

____
____
____
____
____
____

2) Investigate the reasons why **retrieval clues** are important in remembering an event.

____
____
____
____

3) Explain how **context-dependent memory** works if a person loses their keys at home or at work.

____
____
____
____
____
____

4) Compare the differences between **context-dependent memory** and **state-dependent memory**.

____
____
____
____
____
____

5) Analyze the reasons why the **serial position effect** and remembering the first and last items of a misplaced grocery list is a lot easier then remembering items from the middle of that grocery list.

____
____
____
____
____
____

6) Differentiate between the **primacy effect** and the **recency effect** when accessing one's **long-term memory**.

7) Evaluate three reasons why **memory** can become distorted and cause a person to forget things.

8) Draw conclusions as to why memories are subject to **storage decay**.

9) Analyze an example of choice as to how **retrieval failure** of a memory happens due to **proactive interference**.

10) Analyze an example of choice as to how **retrieval failure** of a memory happens due to **retroactive interference**.

11) Investigate a few reasons for the **misinformation effect** when recalling a memory.

12) Formulate a theory as to how **source misattribution** can lead to misleading information about an event.

Name____________________
Period__________________
Date____________________

Cognition-How Your Mind Can Amaze and Betray You: Crash Course Psychology #15

1) Evaluate and explain an example in your own life where YOU made a dumb decision even though YOU are probably pretty intelligent.

____
____
____
____
____
____

2) Analyze how **concept formation** can help people to make sense of the world.

____
____
____
____
____

3) Explain how a person organizes **concepts** and forms **prototypes** by analyzing an example of choice.

____
____
____
____
____
____

4) Why do YOU think it is important to keep an open **mind** and make room for evolving **concepts**?

____
____
____
____
____
____

5) Analyze the ways in which a person's **cognition** works to solve problems.

____
____
____
____
____
____
____

6) Construct an **algorithm** that is logical, has a step-by-step procedure, and guarantees and eventual solution.

____

____

____

____

____

7) Compare an **algorithmic approach** to a **heuristic approach** when solving a problem.

____

____

____

____

8) Provide an example as to how **cognition** can lead a person astray due to their own **confirmation bias**.

____

____

____

____

____

____

9) Critique how **belief perseverance** can cloud a person's judgement. *Provide an example.*

____

____

____

____

____

____

10) Evaluate how a person's **mental set** predisposes how a person thinks and perceives.

____

____

____

____

____

____

11) Clarify the reasons why the **availability heuristic** can warp a person's judgement and why those memories are more likely to be **mentally available**. *(Provide an example)*

____

____

____

____

____

____

____

Name___________________
Period__________________
Date____________________

Language: Crash Course Psychology #16

1) Analyze the way in which body movements, sounds, and thoughts are communicated through **language** from one person's brain to another person's brain.

____
____
____
____

2) Analyze how, even though there are over 7,000 languages, each language can be broken down into a basic structure using the same three building blocks: **phonemes**, **morphemes**, and **grammar**.

____
____
____
____
____
____
____

3) Investigate and report upon the origins of the word **infant**.

____
____
____
____
____

4) Draw conclusions as to how **receptive language** can affect a child who is listening to a conversation between two people. *(Include an example along with your analysis.)*

____
____
____
____
____
____

5) Assess how **productive language** happens when babies start to develop a way to produce their own words.

____
____
____
____
____
____

6) Connect the reasons why a child can lose the ability to both hear and to create particular **tones** and **sounds** of other languages which are not part of the child's home language.

____

____

____

____

7) Compare the way in which **language** progresses from a child who is **12-months-old** to a child who is **18-months-old** to a child who is **two-years-old**.

____

____

____

____

____

8) Explain the "nature vs. nurture," debate between B.F. Skinner (1904-1990) and Noam Chomsky (1928-Present).

____

____

____

____

____

9) Cite evidence to either back up or refute Noam Chomsky's assertion that all human languages contain **universal grammar**.

____

____

____

____

10) Assess how **aphasia** can both impair speaking and understanding of a language.

____

____

____

11) Analyze what happens to a person's speech when **Broca's Area** in the left frontal lobe of the brain is damaged.

____

____

____

____

12) Analyze what happens to a person's speech when **Wernicke's Area** in the left frontal lobe of the brain is damaged.

____

____

____

____

Name____________________
Period___________________
Date____________________

The Power of Motivation: Crash Course Psychology #17

1) Explain the most basic human physical need of **motivation**.

____
____
____
____

2) Analyze the reasons why YOU decided to go to school today and complete the worksheet *The Power of Motivation: Crash Course Psychology #17*.

____
____
____
____
____
____

3) Clarify what paleontologist Steven Jay Gould (1941-2002) meant when he said that behaviors were just "**accidents of evolution**," called **spandrels**.

____
____
____

4) Apprise how people define **instinct** today by explaining the current understanding of **instinct** from an **evolutionary perspective**.

____
____
____
____
____

5) Analyze how **individual experience** plays a major role in **behavior** and **motivation** by explaining the **drive-reduction theory**.

____
____
____
____

6) Draw conclusions as to why YOU are being pulled along by **incentives** by analyzing an example of choice that explains why YOU decided to do something.

____
____
____
____
____

7) Cite evidence as to how the **Optimal Arousal Theory** explains why people are more complicated than just their want to fulfill their **homeostatic systems**.

8) Briefly evaluate the problem of **human motivation** found inside of **Maslow's Hierarchy of Needs Theory** first proposed by Abraham Maslow (1908-1970) inside of his 1943 paper, "A Theory of Human Motivation."

9) Develop a logical argument as to why sex motivates people to do things.

10) Connect how the sensation of hunger motivates people to do things both **physiologically** and **psychologically**.

11) Analyze the results of the **Minnesota Hunger Experiment** (1945) by Ancel Keys (1904-2004) that measured the effects of semi-starvation by partially starving its volunteers.

12) Evaluate the reasons why **social bonding** has helped humans survive throughout time.

Name___________________
Period__________________
Date___________________

The Growth of Knowledge: Crash Course Psychology #18

1) Briefly explain how there are many things which influence YOUR mind and how that influences YOUR **developmental psychology** or perception of the world over time. *(For an extra assignment-think back to a movie that you have seen at least twice and compare how it was different from the first time you saw it in say middle school and then saw it wherever YOU are now. What changed? What stayed the same? Why do you think this happened?*

____
____
____
____
____
____

2) Assess your own **growth of knowledge** by explaining the process in which YOU have matured over the course of the last ten years. *(Feel free to expand upon concrete examples from your own past. A suggestion could show a fear you have overcome, or a change of taste, or a change in type of friend selection.)*

____
____
____
____
____
____

3) Compare the basic similarities between everybody's **developmental psychology** even though everyone grows and matures through a process of **maturation** differently.

____
____
____
____
____
____

4) Connect the reasons that led Jean Piaget (1896-1980) to develop a logical argument in order to explain why the struggle to make sense of our experiences allows us to grow.

____
____
____
____
____
____

5) Analyze the **four-stage theory** of **cognitive development** designed by Jean Piaget in order to describe how we learn at different phases of our lives:

A) **Sensory motor stage** – achievements = object permanence

____

____

____

____

____

B) **Preoperational stage** Part 1 - egocentrism, animism, reversibility struggle, centration

____

____

____

____

C) **Preoperational stage** Part 2 - theory of mind, empathy

____

____

____

____

D) **Concrete Operational Stage** - decentration

____

____

____

____

E) **Formal Operational Stage** - abstract thinking, problem solving

____

____

____

____

6) Differentiate between the competing theories of Piaget and his Russian contemporary Lev Vygotsky (1896-1934).

____

____

____

____

____

____

7) Briefly explain the results of Piaget's greatest conceptual achievement of developing **theoretical depth** in **thinking styles** between kids and adults.

____

____

____

____

____

Name____________________
Period____________________
Date____________________

Monkeys and Morality: Crash Course Psychology #19

1) Why do YOU think that **contact** and **touch** are vital to a person's **psychological development**?

2) Hypothesize as to why **familiarity** is key to attachment.

3) Analyze how the outcome of the experiment of the **strange situation**, created by psychologist Mary Ainsworth (1913-1999), led to the understanding about the importance of a **mother's attentiveness** towards her child in the child's early stages of their **psychological development**.

4) Explain the reasons why **attachment** is vital in building the foundation of **basic trust** between parents and their children.

5) Draw conclusions as to why children who are exposed to **extended abuse**, **trauma**, and **neglect** are at higher risk for experiencing **psychological disorders**, **health problems**, and **substance abuse** as adults.

6) Briefly evaluate how one of the biggest achievements of childhood is achieving a **positive sense** of **self** or **self-concept**.

____

____

____

7) Briefly explain at least one reason why YOU think that kids with **positive self-images** are likely to be happy, confident, independent, and sociable.

____

____

____

8) Analyze the three major **personality styles** of parenting:
   a) **Authoritarian** parent

   ____

   ____

   ____

   b) **Permissive** parent

   ____

   ____

   ____

   c) **Authoritative** parent

   ____

   ____

   ____

9) Analyze how the ability to discern the differences between **right and wrong** and the formation of **individual character** give a person the basis for their **morality**.

____

____

____

____

____

10) Analyze the three basic levels of **moral thinking**:
   a) **Preconventional morality** phase

   ____

   ____

   ____

   b) **Conventional morality** phase

   ____

   ____

   ____

   c) **Postconventional morality** phase

   ____

   ____

   ____

Name___________________
Period__________________
Date___________________

Adolescence: Crash Course Psychology #20

1) Why do YOU think that **teenagers** are so susceptible to **peer pressure**?

____
____
____
____
____

2) Connect the reasons why Erik Erikson (1902-1994) believed that our **personalities** develop in a predetermined order using the **eight-stage model** as reference.

____
____
____
____
____
____
____
____

3) Draw conclusions as to why **teen years** are important to the **psychological growth** of an individual as well as being marked by lots of physical changes.

____
____
____
____
____
____
____

4) Analyze the reasons why Erikson believed that **young adulthood**, or the period of time spanning from one's early 20s to one's early 40s, is marked by the struggle between **intimacy** and **isolation**.

____
____
____
____
____
____
____
____
____
____

5) Apply concepts to understand why many people who lack **established jobs** or their own **family structure** during **middle adulthood** could experience overall boredom or absence of purpose potentially leading to a **mid-life crisis**.

____

____

____

____

____

6) Cite evidence that shows why people who are in stage eight of **late adulthood** (65 and up) look back upon their lives with either **integrity** or **despair**.

____

____

____

____

____

7) Briefly analyze the **physical changes** which occur to somebody over the course of time.

____

____

____

____

8) Compare **fluid intelligence** to **crystallized intelligence**.

____

____

____

____

____

____

____

____

9) Investigate the reasons why some older people will experience a substantial loss of brain cells with serious consequences caused by **dementia**.

____

____

____

____

____

____

10) Why do YOU think that we still have a lot to learn about the aging process?

____

____

____

____

____

Name___________________
Period__________________
Date___________________

Rorschach and Freudians: Crash Course Psychology #21

1) Analyze the similarities and differences between psychoanalyst Hermann Rorschach's (1884-1922) childhood game of **klecksography** and Carl Jung's (1875-1961) **word association** game.

____
____
____
____
____

2) Critique the reasons why some people have been critical of the **Rorschach test** even when other people have believed it to be a good tool in understanding **personality**.

____
____
____
____

3) Explain how psychologists study **personality**.

____
____
____
____
____

4) Briefly analyze the four different types and competing perspectives of **personality theories**.

____
____
____
____
____
____
____

5) Investigate the reasons that led Sigmund Freud (1856-1939) to theorize the existence of the **unconscious** mind and his views of how a person's childhood shapes their **psychoanalytic perspective**.

____
____
____
____
____
____

6) Analyze the interactions between the different parts of the mind which shape a person's **personality**, i.e., the **id**, the **ego**, the **superego**.

____

____

____

____

____

____

____

7) Explain how the defense mechanism of **repression** causes a person to **regress** to habits from an earlier age.

____

____

____

____

____

____

____

8) Analyze how **reaction formation** normally stops a person from punching another person in the face.

____

____

____

____

____

____

9) Explain how **projection** is a way to hide a person's own **negative impulses**.

____

____

____

____

____

____

____

10) Explain how **rationalization** gives excuses for a person's **behavior**.

____

____

____

____

____

____

____

____

11) Analyze how **displacement** works by people to **redirect** their anger.

____
____
____
____
____
____
____

12) Explain how **denial** works against **realistic perception**.

____
____
____
____
____
____
____

13) Analyze the five different **psychosexual stages** in **psychological development** proposed by Sigmund Freud: oral, anal, phallic, latency, and genital.

____
____
____
____
____
____
____
____
____

14) Draw conclusions as to why Abraham Maslow (1908-1970) came to believe that people have five categories of needs in order to promote the growth of **self-actualization**: physiological, safety, love, esteem, and **self-actualization** at the top for meaning in life.

____
____
____
____
____
____
____
____
____
____
____
____
____

Name____________________
Period__________________
Date____________________

Measuring Personality: Crash Course Psychology #22

1) Analyze YOUR p**ersonality**. *Include if YOU are friendly, quirky, maybe creative, or nervous, outgoing or timid, or a combination of these types of personalities. Explain why you are the types of personalities YOU chose with brief examples of YOUR behavior.*

____
____
____
____
____
____

2) Briefly describe a few ways in which people throughout time have chosen to analyze a person's **personality**.

____
____
____
____
____

3) Explain how the **theory of trait perspective** was developed by **psychologists** so that a more **empirical approach** could be taken when analyzing somebody's **psychology**.

____
____
____
____

4) Differentiate between the **Big Five** fundamental characteristics of personality: **openness**, **conscientiousness**, **extroversion**, **agreeableness**, and **neuroticism**. *Use mnemonics to help remember = OCEAN or CANOE.*

____
____
____
____
____
____

5) Explain how understanding the fundamental **characteristics** of somebody's **personality**, e.g., an **introvert** or **extrovert**, works well in **predicting** their **behavior**.

____
____
____
____
____

6) Synthesize what conditions might cause somebody stray away from their core **personality**.

____

____

____

____

7) Explain how the **social cognitive perspective** emphasizes the interaction (aka **reciprocal determinism**) between **traits** and **social context** in our **behavior**.

____

____

____

____

8) Evaluate how the **personal control** of somebody who has an **anxious-suspicious personality** could change if they start having a crush on another person.

____

____

____

____

____

9) Differentiate between a **Thematic Apperception Test** and a **Trait Personality Test**.

____

____

____

____

____

10) Why do YOU think that the **Minnesota Multiphasic Personality Inventory** is a widely used personality test?

____

____

____

11) Draw conclusions around Albert Bandura's (1925-present) **social cognitive camp** and school of thought by analyzing an example of that type of thought.

____

____

____

____

____

12) Assess the reasons why Abraham Maslow (1908-1970) and those who adhere to the **Humanistic Theory** reject **standardized assessments** altogether.

____

____

____

____

Name___________________
Period_________________
Date___________________

Controversy of Intelligence: Crash Course Psychology #23

1) Analyze how the statistical procedure of **factor analysis**, which was developed by psychologist Charles Spearman (1863-1945), determined how certain clusters of skills might have mutual connections with other ones.

____
____
____
____

2) Evaluate how the **G-Factor**, aka general intelligence, was developed during **psychometric** investigations of **cognitive abilities** in order to explain why people who do well on one **cognitive test** tend to do well on others.

____
____
____
____

3) Differentiate between the seven clusters of **mental abilities** outlined by Louis Leon Thurstone (1887-1955): **special ability**, **verbal comprehension**, **word fluency**, **perceptual speed**, **numerical ability**, **inductive reasoning**, and **memory**.

____
____
____
____
____

4) Assess how Howard Gardner (1943-present) viewed **intelligence** as multiple abilities that come in eight different forms: **musica**l, **mathematical**, **linguistic**, **naturalistic**, **interpersonal**, **intrapersonal**, **spatial**, and **kinesthetic abilities**.

____
____
____
____
____
____

5) Analyze the three types of **intelligence** outlined by psychologist Robert Sternberg (1949-present): **analytical** (problem solving) **intelligence**, **creative intelligence**, and **practical intelligence**.

____
____
____
____

6) Critique why **intelligence** measured from **standardized tests** does not account for the **intelligence** found inside of **divergent thinking**.

7) Analyze how the fictional character of **Sherlock Holmes** benefitted from mastering the five main components of **creativity**: expertise, imaginative thinking, a venturesome personality, intrinsic motivation, and a creative environment.

8) Hypothesize a **scenario** where a person's **emotional intelligence** either aids or hinders their ability to perceive, understand, manage, and use emotions.

9) Connect how ideas surrounding **eugenics** in the 19th century was adopted by not only **eugenicists** in the USA but also by the **Nazi party** in Germany in the 20th century.

10) Evaluate how Adolf Hitler (1889-1945) and the Nazis took **eugenics** to its darkest point.

Name____________________
Period___________________
Date____________________

Brains vs. Bias: Crash Course Psychology #24

1) Develop a logical argument as to why the scores of the **Wechsler Adult Intelligence Scale** (WAIS) achievement test is used as the current standard measurement of a person's intelligence.

____
____
____
____

2) Compare the differences between two types of **cognitive tests**: the **achievement test** and the **aptitude test**.

____
____
____
____

3) Apply concepts and explain the three important marks that make an **intelligence test** good: **standardized**, **reliable**, **valid**.

   A) **Standardized**

   ____
   ____
   ____
   ____
   ____

   B) **Reliable**

   ____
   ____
   ____
   ____

   C) **Validity**

   ____
   ____
   ____
   ____

4) Compare the differences between **construct validity** and **criterion validity**.

____
____
____
____
____
____

5) Evaluate why twin and adoption studies have been helpful in illustrating how **intelligence** is influenced by both **genetic** and **environmental** factors.

____

____

____

____

____

6) Compare the differences between the brains of **identical** and **fraternal** twins.

____

____

____

____

____

7) Analyze the research available on the **physical** and **mental aptitude** potential tests that have been done with adopted children, adopted siblings, parents, and biological parents.

____

____

____

____

____

8) Why do YOU think that **life experiences** and **environmental conditions** could possibly play a role in either limiting or expanding a person's **intelligence**?

____

____

____

____

____

9) Investigate and report on the methods J. McVicker Hunt (1906-1991) used to develop an understanding as to how malleable **early childhood intelligence** can be especially in disadvantaged and stressful situations.

____

____

____

____

____

10) Cite evidence as to how a **mental aptitude test** could have **testing bias** towards a certain **race** or **gender**.

____

____

____

____

____

Name____________________
Period___________________
Date_____________________

Feeling all the Feels: Crash Course Psychology #25

1) Explain how **emotions** play an important role in how people think and behave.

____
____
____
____
____

2) Analyze the way in which **emotions** involve **physiological arousal**, **expressive behaviors**, and **conscious experience**.

____
____
____
____
____
____
____

3) Differentiate between psychologists William James (1842-1910) and Carle Lange (1834-1900) who came to the conclusion that **physiological arousal** precedes **emotion**, and the studies of Walter Bradford Cannon (1871-1945) and Philip Bard (1898-1977) who concluded that **bodily responses** and **emotions** occur separately but simultaneously.

____
____
____
____
____
____
____
____

4) Evaluate the **two-factor theory** proposed in the 1960s by psychologists Stanley Schachter (1922-1997) and Jerome Singer (1934-2010) where **cognition** defines **emotion**.

____
____
____
____
____
____
____
____

5) Cite evidence as to how **arousal** can bubble over from one event to the next in what Schachter and Singer called the **spillover effect**.

____
____
____
____
____
____

6) Explain how reading a love letter from YOUR boyfriend or girlfriend could cause mushy feelings in YOUR heart which can be later analyzed by YOUR **cognitive process**.

____
____
____
____
____

7) Investigate and report on the function of the **limbic system** in the human body.

____
____
____
____

8) Compare how memories are made by analyzing how fear responses in the **amygdala** are triggered by the "slow" **high road** and the "fast" **low road** when determining the differences between a stick and a snake.

____
____
____
____

9) Differentiate between the **sympathetic** and **parasympathetic** divisions of a person's **autonomic nervous system**.

____
____
____
____
____
____

10) Compare the differences in **brain activity** between **positive feelings** and **negative feelings**.

____
____
____
____
____
____

Name____________________
Period___________________
Date_____________________

Emotion, Stress, and Health: Crash Course Psychology #26

1) Why do YOU think that people who have a more **positive outlook** on life tend to live longer than people who have a **negative outlook** on life?

____
____
____
____
____

2) Explain the reasons why **facial expressions** are **culturally universal** by taking into account the **facial feedback hypothesis**.

____
____
____
____
____
____

3) Compare the reasons why **introverts** are usually better at interpreting people's feelings than **extroverts**.

____
____
____
____
____

4) Connect why the meaning between a few different **gestures** made by a few different **cultures** may be different.

____
____
____
____
____

5) Analyze how the **two-dimensional model** explains **moral psychology** to show how emotions can be expressed both positively and negatively on a **spectrum**.

____
____
____
____
____
____

6) Evaluate a time in YOUR life in which YOU experienced **stress**. How did you cope with the **stress**? Why was the situation so stressful?

____

____

____

____

____

____

7) Differentiate between the three main categories of **external stressors**:

   a) **Catastrophes**

   ____

   ____

   ____

   b) **Significant life changes**

   ____

   ____

   ____

   c) **Everyday inconveniences**

   ____

   ____

   ____

8) Briefly analyze the reasons why people experience **stress**.

____

____

____

____

____

9) Briefly explain how the **autonomic nervous system** along with the **enteric nervous system** is responsible for **digestive problems**.

____

____

____

____

____

____

____

10) Draw conclusions as to how **stress** could cause **heart disease**.

____

____

____

____

____

____

Name___________________
Period__________________
Date___________________

Let's Talk About Sex: Crash Course Psychology #27

1) Investigate and report on the controversial task researcher Alfred Kinsey (1894-1956) undertook in his scientific study of **human sexuality** to advance the field of **sexology**.

2) Analyze what **sex** has done for **humanity**.

3) Explain how the definition of **gender** differs from the definition of **sex**.

4) Explain the differences between the **physiological** and **psychological** aspects of **sex**.

5) Explain the differences between the four different and distinct stages of **sex**:
   a) **Excitement**

   b) **Plateau**

   c) **Orgasm**

d) **Resolution**

____

____

____

6) Evaluate the function of **hormones**, specifically **sex hormones**, and report on the role they play inside of the **endocrine system**.

____

____

____

____

____

____

____

7) Clarify the differences between **estrogen** and **testosterone**.

____

____

____

____

____

8) Explain how **puberty** affects teenagers and their **libido**.

____

____

____

____

____

9) Analyze why humans need not only **sex hormones** but also the right **psychological** and **visual stimuli** to keep themselves going sexually.

____

____

____

____

____

____

____

10) Explain how **social-cultural influences** such as the **society** a person lives in, their **religion**, and **personal values** can influence the way a person views **sex**.

____

____

____

____

____

____

____

11) Compare the differences between **social-cultural influences**, **external stimuli**, and **internal stimuli**.

____

____

____

____

____

12) Explain the reasons why **human judgment** and **morality** are often entangled with **desire** and **sex**.

____

____

____

____

13) Why do YOU think a number of people used to believe that **masturbation** could be a part of a **mental illness**? (*If YOU still feel that **masturbation** is a **mental illness**, please explain the reasons why you feel this way in your answer here.*)

____

____

____

____

____

14) Explain how somebody's **sexual orientation** is NOT a **mental health** problem. (*If YOU still feel like it is a **mental health problem**, please explain the reasons why YOU feel this way in your answer here.)*

____

____

____

____

____

15) Evaluate whether or not **genetic** or **environmental factors** play a definitive role in one's **sexual orientation**.

____

____

____

____

____

16) Briefly explain why many people choose to be **sexually intimate** with other people.

____

____

____

____

____

____

Name____________________
Period__________________
Date____________________

Psychological Disorders: Crash Course Psychology #28

1) Evaluate what happened during the **psychological experiment** of undercover **pseudo-patients** conducted by psychologist David Rosenhan (1929-2012) and documented in the book On Being in Insane Places (1975).

2) Explain what factors people may think about when they reflect upon **psychology**.

3) Develop an argument in support of the conclusions found by the **World Health Organization** (**WHO**) that over 450 million people suffer from **psychological disorders**.

4) Explain what YOU think about people who exhibit **deviant behavior**. *Include if you support or disapprove of* ***deviant behavior****.*

5) Investigate and report as to how **deviant behavior** could be classified as a **disorder**.

6) Show how **distress** could lead to truly harmful **dysfunction**.

____

____

____

____

____

7) Draw conclusions as to why it took so long to shift to the **Medical Model of Psychological Disorder** and begin thinking about **disorders** as rooted in **science**.

____

____

____

____

____

____

____

8) Explain the **comprehensive method** of the **biopsychological approach** paying close attention as to how it defines **normal behavior** first by filling in the table and then by explaining it.

Biological Influences	Socio-Cultural Influences	Psychological Influences

____

____

____

____

____

____

____

9) Critique the changes of the standardized book on **psychoanalysis** the American Psychiatric Association's Diagnostic and Statistical Manual of Mental Disorders as both **positive** and **negative**.

____

____

____

____

____

____

____

Name___________________
Period_________________
Date___________________

OCD and Anxiety Disorders: Crash Course Psychology #29

1) Clarify what would constitute somebody to be diagnosed with a **psychological disorder**.

____
____
____
____
____

2) Differentiate between **anxiety disorders** and **fear** by analyzing a person's **dysfunctional behavior.**

____
____
____
____
____

3) Show how unwanted **repetitive thoughts** become **obsessions** that would characterize the **condition** known as **obsessive compulsive disorder** (**OCD**).

____
____
____
____
____

4) Briefly explain what type of **treatments** are available for people who suffer from **OCD**.

____
____

5) Explain how somebody who is continually **tense** and **apprehensive**, and who also has unfocused **negative** and out of control **feelings** could be diagnosed with **generalized anxiety disorder** (**GAD**). *Use an example of a **personality** to defend your answer.*

____
____
____
____
____

6) Analyze the way in which **persistent stress** or **psychological trauma** could trigger a **panic disorder** such as a **panic attack**. *Defend your answer an example.*

____
____
____
____
____

7) Draw conclusions as to how **panic attacks** could lead to **avoidance behavior**.

8) Why do YOU think that somebody who has **social anxiety disorder** may find it difficult to interact with others?

9) Evaluate the effectiveness of **reinforcement** in child development during the **social conditioning experiment** of John B. Watson (1878-1958).

10) Briefly explain how **anxiety** could be acquired from other people through **observational learning**.

11) Hypothesize how **natural selection** could play a role in triggering **anxiety**.

12) Analyze how **genetics** and **brain chemistry** could play a role in triggering **anxiety**.

Name___________________
Period_________________
Date___________________

Depressive and Bipolar Disorders: Crash Course Psychology #30

1) Explain how psychologist Dr. Kay Redfield Jamison (1946-present) in her memoir, "An Unquiet Mind," contributed to a greater understanding of the **manic-depressive** mood **disorder** now known as **bipolar disorder**.

____
____
____
____

2) Clarify the differences between **mood** and the **ten basic emotions** of joy, surprise, sadness, anger, contempt, shame, fear, guilt, and disgust.

____
____
____
____

3) Clarify the differences between **moods** and **mood disorders** such as **depressive disorders** and **bipolar disorder**.

____
____
____
____
____

4) Analyze how **depression** is both a **physiological** and **psychological** illness.

____
____
____
____
____

5) Explain how a clinically **depressed** person may have trouble living a normal life. *Defend your answer with examples.*

____
____
____
____

6) Explain why full-blown **manic episodes** can often lead an individual needing **psychiatric hospitalization**.

____
____
____
____

7) Clarify how **mood disorders** are often a combination of **biological** and **genetic** factors.

8) Clarify how **mood disorders** are often a combination of **psychological** and **environmental** factors.

9) Explain how the naturally occurring drug **norepinephrine** plays a role in either exaggerating or limiting **arousal** and focus inside of the brain.

10) Explain how exercising can increase **serotonin** levels and aid in alleviating the **symptoms** of **depression**.

11) Evaluate the merits of looking at **depressive** and **bipolar disorders** from a **Social-Cognitive** perspective. *Defend your argument with an example.*

Name____________________
Period__________________
Date____________________

Trauma and Addiction: Crash Course Psychology #31

1) Connect how **Post-traumatic stress disorder** (**PTSD**) can manifest itself in nightmares, flashbacks, avoidance, fear, guilt, anxiety, rage, and insomnia.

____
____
____
____
____
____

2) Develop a logical argument as to why many **PTSD** patients may experience **numbing** or periods of being **emotionless** and **disconnected** with their surrounding reality.

____
____
____
____
____

3) Explain what happens when any of the **disorders** manifested due to **PTSD** are left untreated.

____
____
____
____
____

4) Assess how **addiction** and **trauma** can go hand in hand and lead to **substance abuse** in order to cope with the **psychological** pain of **PTSD**.

____
____
____
____
____
____

5) Clarify the differences between **fear conditioning** and **moral injury** by analyzing an example of somebody suffering from PTSD in the military.

____
____
____
____
____

6) Draw conclusions as to why **genetic predisposition** may make some people more vulnerable than others towards **PTSD**.

____

____

____

____

7) Draw conclusions as to why **context** and **environment** may make some people more vulnerable than others towards **PTSD**.

____

____

____

____

____

8) Apply concepts and explain how **PTSD** symptoms share some similarities with **anxiety disorders** taking into account how different parts of the brain react to **trauma**.

____

____

____

____

____

____

9) Explain how somebody with **PTSD** can have **post-traumatic growth** involving positive **psychological** changes.

____

____

____

____

10) Critique the problems some people face when **self-medicating** in order to deal with their problems and how this could lead to **addiction** or **dependence** on drugs, alcohol, or sex in order to relieve **negative emotions**. *Expand upon an example of choice.*

____

____

____

____

____

____

11) Do YOU think that **addiction** is a mental illness, a physical disease, or perhaps a combination of both? *Defend your answer.*

____

____

____

____

____

Name____________________
Period__________________
Date____________________

Schizophrenia and Dissociative Disorders: Crash Course Psychology #32

1) Briefly explain the major **misconceptions** between **schizophrenia** and **dissociative identify disorder**. *Be sure to explain why the two are often mixed up.*

____

____

____

____

____

2) Examine the **chronic condition disorder** of **schizophrenia**. *Include how the **psychotic symptoms** of **schizophrenia** manifest themselves inside of adults.*

____

____

____

____

____

____

3) Explain the eight major hallmarks of people diagnosed with **classic schizophrenia** by including examples of the following:
   a) **Loss of contact** with **reality**

   ____

   ____

   b) **Psychotic symptoms**

   ____

   ____

   c) **Disorganized thinking** & **speech**

   ____

   ____

   d) Breakdown in **selective attention**

   ____

   ____

   e) **Delusions** or **false beliefs**

   ____

   ____

   f) Narratives of **persecution** and **paranoia**

   ____

   ____

   g) **Perceptual disturbances** (hallucinations)

   ____

   ____

h) **Disorganized** and **abnormal emotions**

4) Explain the three major categories of **psychotic symptoms** using examples:
   a) **Positive symptoms**

   b) **Negative symptoms**

   c) **Disorganized symptoms**

5) Explain the **physiological predisposition** some people have towards **schizophrenia**. *Include how **dopamine** plays a role in **schizophrenic** patients.*

6) Draw conclusions as to how it is believed that the **thalamus** and **amygdala** areas of the brain play a major role in people diagnosed with **schizophrenia** in the **diathesis-stress model**.

7) Analyze and explain an experience people with **dissociative disorders** or **disorders of consciousness** may experience.

8) Evaluate the accuracy of the **Sybil case** where a woman claimed to have **Dissociative Identity Disorder** (**DID**) or **Multiple Personality Disorder**.

Name____________________
Period___________________
Date_____________________

Eating and Body Dysmorphic Disorders: Crash Course Psychology #33

1) Explain what happens to somebody when they suffer from **Anorexia Nervosa**, a disorder of the mind.

____
____
____
____
____

2) Why do YOU think **eating disorders** have been increasing since the 1950s?

____
____
____
____
____

3) Explain the three main categories of **eating disorders** along with their **symptoms**:

   a) **Anorexia** (refusing to eat)

   ____
   ____
   ____
   ____
   ____
   ____
   ____

   b) **Bulimia (**secretly **binge-purge**)

   ____
   ____
   ____
   ____
   ____
   ____
   ____
   ____

   c) **Binge-eating** (eating large amounts of food in a short period of time)

   ____
   ____
   ____
   ____
   ____
   ____

4) Evaluate the **standard ideal** of beauty portrayed by the media today, and how that can warp a person's **perception** as to what is or isn't beautiful.

____

____

____

____

____

5) Explain how getting **plastic surgery** to look like a barbie doll or a famous celebrity is an example of **body dysmorphic disorder**.

____

____

____

____

____

6) Analyze the **symptoms** that a person who suffers from **Obsessive-Compulsive Disorder** (**OCD**) along with **Body Dysmorphic Disorder** (**BDD**) might experience.

____

____

____

____

____

____

7) Formulate a **hypothesis** as to why some **bodybuilders** suffer from **muscle dysmorphia**.

____

____

____

____

____

8) Draw conclusions as to how an imbalance of brain chemicals inside of **neurotransmitters** such as **serotonin** and **dopamine** may cause **eating** and **body dysmorphic disorders** (**BDD**).

____

____

____

____

____

____

9) Draw conclusions using the **biological model** as to why people may be **genetically** predisposed to **BDD**

____

____

____

____

Name____________________
Period__________________
Date____________________

Personality Disorders: Crash Course Psychology #34

1) Analyze the differences between **ego-dystonic** and **ego-syntonic**.

____
____
____
____
____
____

2) Explain how a **personality disorder** can impair one's **social skills**. (*e.g. **narcissism**, lack of **empathy***)

____
____
____
____
____

3) Develop a logical argument as to why people find **personality disorders** such as **psychopathy** and **sociopathy** to be so scary.

____
____
____
____
____

4) Plot 10 **personality disorders** based on how they are related using the chart below. Then briefly explain why YOU grouped each **personality disorder** in three different clusters: **Paranoid**, **obsessive-compulsive**, **schizoid**, **antisocial**, **histrionic**, **avoidant**, **borderline**, **narcissistic**, **dependen**t, **schizotypal**.

Cluster A	Cluster B	Cluster C

Cluster A:

____
____
____

Cluster B:

____
____
____

Cluster C:

____

____

____

5) Analyze and explain how a **dimensional model** functions in helping to categorize **personality disorders**.

____

____

____

____

6) Cite evidence as to how a person with **borderline personality disorder** (**BPD**) behaves.

____

____

____

____

____

7) Show how men with **Antisocial Personality Disorder** can exhibit a **lack of conscience** when they do something wrong. *Include some famous examples.*

____

____

____

____

____

8) Analyze how one's response to normal childhood fears could signal **psychopathic behavior** later in life. *Use the conditional tense in your answer, e.g., "if".*

____

____

____

____

9) Evaluate what happens when a person with **psychopathic** personality features has the **neural basis** of their **antisocial disorder** stimulated with evocative photographs.

____

____

____

____

10) Draw conclusions surrounding the **PET** (**Positron emission tomography**) scan results of people who are considered to have a **normal brain** and compare the results with those who have been **convicted of murder**.

____

____

____

____

____

Name____________________
Period__________________
Date____________________

Getting Help: Crash Course Psychology #35

1) Point out and examine the benefits of receiving a **Sigmund Freud** (1856-1939) type of **psychotherapy** in order to overcome **repressed feelings** and achieve **personal growth**.

2) Explain how some **therapists** use a technique known as **psychoanalysis** in order to point out **unconscious** themes such as **resistance** in a patient's speech.

3) Briefly analyze the relationship between **psychoanalysis** and **psychodynamic**.

4) Explain the four major schools of **psychotherapy**:
   a) **Psychodynamic**

   b) **Existential-humanistic**

   c) **Behavioral**

   d) **Cognitive**

5) Draw conclusions as to why a **humanistic therapist** would choose to provide **client-centered therapy** for their clients.

6) Explain the ideas behind providing **existential-humanistic therapy** for somebody with **depression**.

7) Cite evidence to support the rationale behind a **behavior therapist** providing **therapy** for somebody who may be **afraid of flying**.

8) Develop a logical argument behind using the **Socratic** questioning method that **cognitive therapist Aaron Beck** (1921-present) designed in order to help somebody who may have **self-defeating thoughts**.

9) Evaluate the benefits behind **group therapy** in aiding **clients** to understand the **therapeutic** benefits of not being alone.

Name____________________
Period__________________
Date____________________

Biomedical Treatments: Crash Course Psychology #36

1) Identify and explain the challenges that psychologists face when trying to determine whether or not **psychotherapy** is working on their patient by evaluating the **self-serving biases** between **client perception**, **clinician perception**, and **outcome research**.
   A) **client perception**
      ____
      ____
      ____
   B) **clinician perception**
      ____
      ____
      ____
   C) **outcome research**
      ____
      ____
      ____

2) Evaluate the ways in which psychologists can objectively measure to see if their **psychotherapy sessions** are working on a patient by **treatment outcome research**.
   ____
   ____
   ____
   ____
   ____
   ____
   ____

3) Differentiate between **effectiveness** and **efficacy**.
   ____
   ____
   ____
   ____

4) Compare the common factors that show which types of **psychotherapy** work the best.
   ____
   ____
   ____
   ____
   ____
   ____
   ____

5) Differentiate between **psychotherapy** and **biomedical therapy**.

____
____
____
____
____
____

6) Analyze the four major categories of **psychotropic drugs** found in **pharmacotherapy**:
   a) **Antipsychotics** (Abilify, Clozaril, Zyprexa, Risperdal, Trilafon, Haldol)

   ____
   ____
   ____
   ____

   b) **Anxiolytics** (Xanax, Librium, Valium, Atarax, Buspar)

   ____
   ____
   ____
   ____

   c) **Antidepressants** (Celexa, Prozac, Cymbalta, Anafranil) (SSRI's=Zoloft, Paxil, Prozac)

   ____
   ____
   ____
   ____

   d) **Mood stabilizers** (Lithium, Lamictal, Tegretol, Depakote)

   ____
   ____
   ____
   ____

7) Evaluate the theories surrounding the success of **electro-shock therapy**, aka **electroconvulsive therapy** (ECT), on a person who is resistant to mood stabilizing drugs.

____
____
____
____
____
____

8) Hypothesize how **repetitive transcranial magnetic stimulation** (rTMS) and **Deep-Brain Stimulation** (DBS) work in treating the brain and mind.

____
____
____
____

Name____________________
Period__________________
Date____________________

Social Thinking: Crash Course Psychology #37

1) Explain how **social psychology** focuses on the power of the situation to examine how people think about, influence, and relate to one another in certain conditions. *Defend your answer through the use of examples.*

____

____

____

____

____

2) Differentiate how the **Attribution Theory**, developed by Fritz Heider (1896-1988), attempts to explain why somebody's behavior is **dispositiona**l or **situational**.

____

____

____

____

____

3) Hypothesize how the internal factors of overestimating somebody's **personality** while underestimating the power of the **situation** can lead to **fundamental attribution error**.

____

____

____

____

____

4) Assess the reasons why a person's **political views** are likely to be strongly influenced by whether or not a person decides to attribute poverty or homelessness to **personal dispositions**.

____

____

____

____

____

5) Analyze how the **Central Route Persuasion** technique, developed by Richard Petty (1937-present) and John Cacioppo (1951-2018) in the late 1970s and 1980s, occurs when a person is persuaded by the content of a message.

____

____

____

____

____

6) Formulate a theory as to why YOU think **Peripheral Route Persuasion** is especially effective in persuading people to buy things or do things, e.g., TV, ads, billboards.

7) Connect the phrase, "fake it till you make it," to how a person's **attitude** can affect their **behavior**.

8) Explain how the **foot-in-the-door** phenomenon can butter people up to make them more likely to comply with a big request.

9) Analyze how the **Stanford Prison Experiment** (1971), conducted by Philip Zimbardo (1933-present), works in order to understand **situational behavior**.

10) Apply concepts to understand why individuals will seek consistency among their beliefs and opinions as suggested in the **Theory of Cognitive Dissonance** by Leon Festinger (1919-1989). *Defend why this is one of the most important concepts in **psychology**.*

Name____________________
Period__________________
Date____________________

Social Influence: Crash Course Psychology #38

1) Analyze the results of the **Milgram Experiment** in the 1960s, led by psychologist Stanley Milgram (1933-1984), that focused on the **social psychology** of obedience and what the average person might be capable of doing when under orders.

____
____
____
____
____
____
____

2) Explain the two key cornerstone topics of **social psychology**:
   a) **Social influence** (Automatic mimicry)

   ____
   ____
   ____
   ____

   b) **Conformity** (matching behaviors to social norms)

   ____
   ____
   ____
   ____

3) Investigate and report on how psychologist Solomon Ash (1907-1996) expressed the power of **conformity** by making the participant feel **incompetent** through a simple test on **visual perception**.

____
____
____
____
____
____

4) Evaluate how **extraneous factors** could cause a participant to question their own **logic** against that of the group.

____
____
____
____
____
____

5) Explain how a people from a certain **culture** tend to conform more to their home culture when emphasis is placed on **social standards**. *Cite examples of groups that may **peer pressure** an individual into following the **social norm**.*

6) Assess what the idea of **normative social influence** reveals about the reasons why people conform to the will of others.

7) Why do YOU think that **social facilitation** allows certain people perform better in front of a group?

8) Formulate a theory as to why **social loafing** can occur in groups and cause **deindividualization** when each person in the group is NOT held accountable.

9) Explain how the **internet** has the ability to strongly enhance **group polarization** by connecting like-minded people.

10) Briefly analyze an example of choice as to how **groupthink** can get people too caught up in the logic of their own group to see things clearly and rationally.

Name___________________
Period__________________
Date____________________

Prejudice and Discrimination: Crash Course Psychology #39

1) Draw conclusions as to how **implicit bias** caused the death of Amadou Diallo (1976-1999) at the hands of police officers in New York in the front of his apartment building.

____
____
____
____
____
____

2) Analyze a time in which YOU believe that YOU were unfairly judged or felt **prejudiced** against in any way. *Why do you think it happened the way it did? Reflect upon and write down your story,* i.e., your age, race, gender, sexual orientation, stereotype.

____
____
____
____
____
____
____
____

3) Explain why YOU think **prejudicial attitudes** are often directed along the lines of **gender**, **ethnic**, **socioeconomic status**, or **culture**.

____
____
____
____
____
____

4) Differentiate between **prejudice**, **stereotyping**, and **discrimination**.

____
____
____
____
____
____
____
____
____
____

5) Cite an example as to how a **prejudice** somebody may have could cross the line and become **discrimination**.

____
____
____
____
____

6) Explain the ways in which **prejudice** can be both **non-conscious** and **automatic**.

____
____
____
____
____

7) Connect the reasons why the **Implicit Association Test** (IAT) was implemented in the late 1990s.

____
____
____
____
____

8) Explain the factors that determine whether a person has an **implicit association bias** towards other people or not.

____
____
____
____
____
____

9) Why do YOU think that a large number of people are **prejudiced**?

____
____
____
____
____
____

10) Evaluate the reasons why dividing the world into **in groups** and **out groups** drives **discrimination**.

____
____
____
____
____
____

Name___________________
Period__________________
Date___________________

Aggression vs. Altruism: Crash Course Psychology #40

1) Analyze the ways in which Muzar Sharif (1906-1988) conducted his **Realistic Conflict Theory** at Robber's Cave with two groups of boys in order to see what happens when you combine negative prejudices with competition over resources. *Do you agree with his methods and testing procedures? Why or why not? Defend your answer.*

____
____
____
____
____
____
____

2) Develop a logical argument as to where **aggression** originates and why people choose to **aggress** verbally, emotionally, and physically.

____
____
____
____
____

3) Connect how there is a link between **aggression** and diminished activity in the **frontal lobes** of the brain.

____
____
____
____
____

4) Explain how a person's **aggression** can be influenced by their own **biochemistry**.

____
____
____
____
____

5) Analyze the **Frustration-Aggression Theory** by comparing it to the sport of baseball.

____
____
____
____
____
____

6) Assess an example of how **altruism**, or self-sacrificing oneself for the welfare of others, works in practice.

____

____

____

____

7) Critique the **bystander effect** and how it can weaken our instinct for **altruism**.

____

____

____

____

____

____

8) Evaluate the reasons why **self-interest** plays a key role in a person's decision to help out another person following the **cost-benefit analysis** scenario.

____

____

____

____

____

____

9) Connect why many people act **altruistically** due to their belief in the **social exchange theory** where the idea is to maximize benefits and minimize costs.

____

____

____

____

____

____

10) Connect why many people act **altruistically** by involving themselves in the **reciprocity norm** so that if something bad ever happens to them, then the idea of **karma** will make sure they are helped out too.

____

____

____

____

____

11) Develop a logical argument that defends why a parent would adhere to the **social-responsibility norm** when deciding whether or not to help out their child.

____

____

____

____

EXTRA ESSAYS SECTION

1) Climate Change
2) The Germaphobe
3) The Control Freak
4) Girl Interrupted
5) The Religious Zealot
6) The PANDAS Child
7) The Astronaut
8) The Policeman
9) The Teacher
10) The Businessman
11) The Ex-Football Player
12) The Piano Teacher
13) The Emotional You

Climate Change

YOU are a psychologist dealing daily with patients who have specific issues. One of YOUR patients Donald is severely depressed and possibly suicidal over recent climate reports. Reflect upon the topic of **climate change** and predict how you would treat somebody who was dealing with thoughts of hopelessness and despair linked to **global warming**. *Defend your thesis and introduction paragraph by including and explaining key terms of psychology throughout your essay.*

“The Germaphobe”

YOU are a psychologist dealing daily with patients who have specific issues. One of YOUR patients Howard has been diagnosed with **Obsessive Compulsive Disorder** (OCD). Howard is a doctor who writes on his statement that he is such a **germaphobe** that he has to keep washing his hands for hours after surgery or else he starts having feelings of **anxiety**. Write a report as to how you would help Howard overcome his **germaphobia**.

- Fear of being contaminated by germs, dirt, and contaminating others.

"The Control Freak"

YOU are a psychologist dealing daily with patients who have specific issues. One of YOUR patients Neil has an **Obsessive-Compulsive Disorder** (**OCD**) where he has to be in control or else he has a meltdown. He gets extremely agitated if something is moved around in his room or not in the right place without his permission to do so. Write a report as to how you would help that person to stop being such a "control freak."

- Fear of losing control and harming themselves

"Girl Interrupted"

YOU are a psychologist dealing daily with patients who have specific issues. One of YOUR patients Susanna has an **Obsessive-Compulsive Disorder** (**OCD**) where she constantly has unwanted violent thoughts of how to kill herself. Her moods are like tides, come in waves, and she has been diagnosed with **Borderline Personality Disorder** along with **OCD**. Write a report as to how you would help Susanna deal with her personality in a non-violent way.

- Intrusive sexually explicit or violent thoughts and images

"The Religious Zealot"

YOU are a psychologist dealing daily with patients who have specific issues. One of YOUR patients Jeanette has an **Obsessive-Compulsive Disorder** (**OCD**) where she is so consumed by religion that there are religious artifacts scattered everywhere in the house. She writes on her initial statement that she is having trouble keeping her friends. She would like to be able to make new friends but doesn't understand how her obsession with religion may be causing her to miss out on opportunities to make new friends. Write a report as to how you would help that person learn how to "mellow out" with her obsession over religion.

- Excessive focus on religious or moral ideas

"The PANDAS Child"

YOU are a psychologist dealing daily with patients who have specific issues. One of YOUR child patients Jimmy has been diagnosed with a rare disease called PANDAS following a strep infection. Jimmy begins throwing items around YOUR therapy room and pretty much having a meltdown during your first hour-long session. Jimmy's parents have reported hitting and biting at home as well as strong **separation anxiety**, **isolationist behavior**, and **eating disorders**. Research PANDAS and then write a report as to how you would advise his parents to help Jimmy deal with his anxiety, anger, and frustration over relatively simple tasks.

"The Astronaut"

YOU are a psychologist dealing daily with patients who have specific issues. NASA recently conducted an experiment on twins Scott and Mark Kelly to observe the effects (**physiological**, **psychological**, and **cognitive**) that could happen to a human from long-term exposure to hazards in space.

YOU are the psychologist dealing with Scott (the twin in space for a year) and helping him postflight after his return to earth. A diagnostic of his post flight tests report that he is experiencing some **memory loss** and both the speed and accuracy of his answers could use some improvement while he is transitioning back to life on earth. He also is slightly depressed that his body is not as strong as it was prior to his trip to space and he reports feeling off when participating in sports (*make up a sport of choice that Scott is having trouble in*).

Write a psychology report as to how you would help Scott re-accustom himself back to life on Earth after being in space for 520 days.

"The Policeman"

YOU are a psychologist dealing daily with patients who have specific issues. One of your patients Frank is very depressed and suffers from **Post-Traumatic Stress Disorder** (**PTSD**). He served in the army for two years prior to his job as a policeman for the last two years. He reports **mood** and **anxiety** problems which are affecting his job as a policeman. Research the causes and effects of depression in patients with **PTSD** and then write a report as to how you would aid your patient in overcoming his **depression**.

"The Teacher"

YOU are a psychologist dealing daily with patients who have specific issues. One of your patients Erin, who is a teacher, is very depressed. She is unhappy and reports a toxic environment at the school site where she works at and reports that many teachers have already quit during the school year. Class sizes have doubled since she started as a teacher five years ago and she is now teaching four different preparation periods. Her administrators have begun to give her negative reviews even though she reports she was once a star teacher at the school. She is trying to make sense of how her dream job turned into a nightmare, especially after YOU help her realize that she is a victim of **gaslighting** by her administrators. Research the causes and effects of this **work-related depression** and then write a report as to how you would aid your patient in overcoming her **depression**.

"The Businessman"

YOU are a psychologist dealing daily with patients who have specific issues. One of your patients Andrew is very depressed. He is unhappy with his job in a company, especially since his workday has increased from eight to twelve-hour days five days a week. Sometimes he even has to work on Saturdays. Even though he doesn't like the hours, he is unwilling to leave his job due to his emotional attachment with his colleagues. He recently asked for a raise but was denied furthering his moody behavior. He reports not being able to find happiness anymore and has lost most of his outlets he used to have when he worked an eight-hour day. Research the causes and effects of **work-related depression** and then write a report as to how you would aid your patient in overcoming his **depression**.

"The Ex-Football Player"

YOU are a psychologist dealing daily with patients who have specific issues. One of your patients Jerry, who used to be a college football player, is reporting that he is experiencing anxiety attacks and confidence problems even though he never had issues with these types of problems before. The **anxiety attacks** are so bad that it is affecting his performance at work, his relationship with his wife and his children, and he reports difficulty sleeping. He also reports crying for no reason at random times as well as **anger issues**. He currently works as a social worker and works daily with hi-risk youth. Research the causes of what YOU believe to be the cause of his **anxiety attacks** and then write a report as to how you would aid your patient in overcoming his **anxiety** and **anger issues**.

"The Piano Teacher"

YOU are a psychologist dealing daily with patients who have specific issues. One of YOUR patients Greta has been diagnosed with an **Obsessive-Compulsive Disorder** (**OCD**). Symptoms include a constant fear that she will not have the things she needs so she keeps checking and rechecking all of her items in her purse over and over again in order to make sure she has everything. She reports that her behavior is affecting her job as a piano teacher. Write a report as to how you would help that person relax over her obsession over losing and not having the things she needs.

- Fear of losing or not having the things they may need

"The Emotional YOU"

Recount a story in which YOU were motivated by **emotions** to make a decision to be bold or be overly cautious or feel embarrassed. *Explain why YOUR emotions made you feel this way. Look back to the guiding questions and bolded vocabulary in Chapter #25 to help you with your vocabulary and terminology.*

EXTRA JOURNAL PAGES

EXTRA JOURNAL PAGES

More books from Pengi Inc.

Other Crash Course workbooks written by Roger Morante and available on Amazon as of 2019.

- Crash Course US History: A Study Guide of Worksheets for US History (2018)
- Crash Course World History: A Study Guide of Worksheets for World History (2018)
- Crash Course Government and Politics: A Study Guide of Worksheets for Government and Politics (2018)
- Crash Course Economics: A Study Guide of Worksheets for Economics (2019)
- Crash Course Literature: A Study Guide of Worksheets for Literature (2019)

Follow me on my public Facebook page for sneak peaks of upcoming books as well updates at: rogermorante@rogermorante13

Made in the USA
Middletown, DE
27 May 2020